Failure Is Not an Option

Failure Is Not an Option

*Step-by-Step Guide
to Make Money Online!*

Carl Kettenacker
Elite Marketer

Copyright © 2016 by Carl Kettenacker.

ISBN: Softcover   978-1-5144-5199-1
          eBook   978-1-5144-5198-4

All rights reserved. No part of this book may be reproduced or transmitted in any form or by any means, electronic or mechanical, including photocopying, recording, or by any information storage and retrieval system, without permission in writing from the copyright owner.

The opinions expressed in this manuscript are solely the opinions of the author and do not represent the opinions or thoughts of the publisher. The author represents and warrants full ownership and/or legal right to publish all the materials in this book.

Any people depicted in stock imagery provided by Thinkstock are models, and such images are being used for illustrative purposes only.
Certain stock imagery © Thinkstock.

Print information available on the last page.

Rev. date: 01/20/2016

To order additional copies of this book, contact:
Xlibris
1-888-795-4274
www.Xlibris.com
Orders@Xlibris.com
729526

CONTENTS

Introduction/Foreword:

    Why You Should Consider a Home-Based Business Part Time or Full Time vii

Chapter 1

    What Are the Advantages of an Online Business at Home 1

Chapter 2

    A Summary of Tools Needed to Start a Home-Based Business 3

Chapter 3

    How to Choose a Product or Service to Promote as Your Offer....11

Chapter 4

    Picking a Domain and Hosting Account 14

Chapter 5

    Why You Need an Autoresponder 16

Chapter 6

    Starting a Campaign 18

Chapter 7

    Your Why Is a Very Important Part of Your Goals 20

Chapter 8

    Tracking and Measurement—So Important.............................22

Chapter 9

    Traffic Sources—Main Stay of Any Campaign.........................24

Chapter 10

    Know Your Customer..28

Chapter 11

    How to Set Up a Campaign 30

Chapter 12

    Pitfalls You Must Avoid 34

Chapter 13

    Final Thoughts Before You Get Started...................................38

BOOK SUMMARY 41

Introduction/Foreword:

Why You Should Consider a Home-Based Business Part Time or Full Time

Welcome to the best industry on the planet! Yes, online marketing is, by far, the most interesting *home business* you can get into for low cost and no financial risk to speak of. People today, notwithstanding the downturn in the economic picture in the USA and the world economy, are looking for "secondary" incomes to supplement their annual salaries, and if you find the right opportunity, you will be able to quit your eight-to-five job completely. In online marketing, like any business opportunity, you need to learn the basics and how to apply them correctly in your campaigns. This is what I will be talking about throughout this book!

Welcome aboard!

Chapter 1

What Are the Advantages of an Online Business at Home

Marketers who have an online business or home business have been surveyed, and these are the points they all came up with:

- You are your own boss. You can either choose to work full time or part time developing your business. It's your decision based upon your needs.
- Low to no financial risk. You can start a home-based business usually for under $1,000. Compare that with the cost of starting a normal business with all kinds of start-up costs, which could run you in the thousands.
- You can offer, in many cases, products that are not found in retail and at the same time learn "online marketing."
- Amazing tax advantage. Remember this saying about taxing, "The system will make you poor or make you rich"? Which do you prefer? There are many advantages you can take of if you have your business set up as an LLC. Way too many advantages to talk about but your account will know all of them. Just to mention one . . . you can take losses against income going back two years and you can carry forward for twenty years losses. (How cool is that?)
- You have no restrictions on the hours you want to work—you set your own hours.

- Amazing market potential. A trillion dollars is spent annually. **wow.**
- No restrictions on who can join your business opportunity. In fact, I recently went to a summit and met a ninety-three-year-old man doing online marketing and doing it well!
- Majority of the programs with online marketing have in-house training. However, later in the book, I will give you my thoughts about training and the necessary tools needed for successful campaigns.
- Even though I can't guarantee you will make any income with online marketing, I know quite a few marketers making between $5,000 and $25,000 per month, and many are making six-figure annual incomes. Look forward to talking more about this later on in the book.
- Freedom is one of the coolest things with online marketing. This means you can have the lifestyle you dreamed of and make it happen!
- With the economy in bad shape, online marketing could boost your income and get you on the path to early retirement!

Now I want to make you aware of the negative thoughts you may hear from your friends and business associates. There is a reason that I am bringing this up at this point. I don't want you to be influenced by "negative thoughts" because negatives thoughts can sway your focus and vision on how good a home-based business can be. In fact, any negative thoughts with any business will harm your focus and prevent you from reaching your potential success.

You may hear comments like these:

- Way too high investment.
- Too much time required.
- Way too much risk for you.
- You don't know anything about a home-based business.

Word of advice: Forget any comments like the above and focus on your vision and what your dreams are for the future!

Chapter 2

A Summary of Tools Needed to Start a Home-Based Business

Before I begin to give you the tools you will need on starting your home-based business, I want to summarize what starting a home-based business is all about.

Like any business start-up, you will have some costs associated with forming your business. However, these start-up costs are usually a lot "lower" than starting up, for example, a lawn-mowing business. You usually won't have insurance costs, inventory parts, rent, people, utilities, phone, and the list goes on.

You will need three things

1. Choosing the right program or company
2. Choosing the right product or service
3. Getting the right training and tools required

Sounds like a normal business? Well, in many ways, it is, but here is how I define it: *Normal business*—you are dealing with people, products, and services. *Home-based business*—you are developing relationships with your prospects and customers by telling stories. Sounds silly but it really works!

It is quite rewarding building relationships with customers and prospects, and what a relief it is not listening to your boss telling you all the things you are doing wrong. In fact, I could be fired unless I straightened up!

How would you like to fire your boss? Many marketers do exactly that after they get their home-based business going great guns!

Now before we get started on the tools you will need, let's take a quiz. This is not a quiz to determine how smart you are but to give you a better understanding of "how a potential prospect feels about a sales presentation."

I am going to give you ten items, and I want you to rank them from 1 to 10 in how you feel they are important to a prospect. Just put the number you feel is the most important to a prospect (that would be number 1) and the least important (being number 10). For everything else, do the same, like second most important and then the third most important until you have done all ten. Do them in pencil, so if you need to erase, you can. I will also give you the answers from the actual prospects after you take the quiz. **NO PEEKING AT THE ANSWERS.** This exercise is only to show you how prospects may differ from your thoughts.

Remember to rank these questions 1–10, 1 being the most important to a prospect in your mind and 10 being the least important in your mind. These questions are not in any order, so don't think they have some value on the quiz.

How important do you consider . . .

- Company's literature
- Company's marketing plan with potential earnings
- Training provided
- Who gave the presentation
- Product line
- Company's management experience
- Company support
- Company image

- Sales kit provided
- Reputation of being first in the business

Did you rank the ten quiz questions 1–10, 1 being the most important and 10 being the least important? I am sure you will be amazed just like I was when I took the same quiz! The purpose of doing this is so you can see the difference on how people "think" based upon what side of the fence they are on, meaning whether you are the seller or buyer! Growing up people will have some embedded opinions already in their mind that will have to be changed while doing a home-based business, but most of that will be covered later in the book.

Now turn the page for the correct answers.

Here are the answers to the ten-question quiz in real importance from the prospect's point of view.

1. *Who gave the presentation*—People don't join companies; they join people.
2. *Support*—People or prospects want to know if there is support for their problems.
3. *Training provided*—People are not worried about commissions yet but whether they will be trained.
4. *Marketing plan/Potential earnings*—People want to know two things: Will they make money? And will "you" help them make money?
5. *Product line*—People want to know whether can they use the products and will the prospects want to buy these products.
6. *Being first in the business*—People want to know if the business will still be around in five to ten years.
7. *Company literature*—People only want to know if literature is available—nothing else.
8. *Company image*—Another big surprise here, people only want to know if the business is legitimate—no interest in fancy offices or buildings.

9. *Sales kit provided*—People only want to know if they had sales material they could use in their business.
10. *Company management experience*—Here is another big surprise, people only want to know if management is friendly, helpful, and has a vision for the future and are like normal people.

Did you like the ten-question quiz? I am sure, just like me, you were surprised by the "rankings" of the questions on what the prospects felt versus what you and I felt gives you a feeling about how customers think what is important to them.

Now let's look at the tools you will need:

Domain—You will need to get a domain set up for your business, especially if you are going to have a website. I use and recommend GoDaddy. It will cost you about $13 per year, and you will need it for connecting your campaigns, websites, and tracking. When picking a domain, use a catchy phrase with some sort of connection to either your campaign you want to run or your LLC business. You will need to have about twelve names written down because many of your domain names could be taken. I prefer .com and .org because these are the most recognizable to prospects and customers.

Hosting—I recommend you use GoDaddy as your hosting company. That way, you can have your domain hosted by the same company, and support is a lot better for questions. Hosting is a way for your domain to be pointed in the right direction for your campaigns. GoDaddy is great on explanation on these two features.

Autoresponder—You are probably wondering what is this and why do you need this service. An autoresponder (A/R) does a couple of really neat things for your campaigns: It helps you build a list of people (prospects) you can market additional offers to, in addition to your current campaign. You also will be able to send follow messages of "content" to your prospects, something of value they can use, helping you develop relationships and branding yourself as a person of authority! You can also use it as a blog or newsletter, very handy tool (a must)! Even though it may sound complicated, it is not, so don't worry about this tool. Most all of the autoresponder companies have great training videos showing you how their autoresponder works, along with great support for your questions. Finding an autoresponder is easy. Just Google autoresponders and pick one you like. There are free ones, but look out for how many prospects you can add to your list, and then there are ones that cost more money but offer more advantages. I use GetResponse for my personal autoresponder because of the additional features it offers. You can expect to pay $15 a month and up to $150 a month, depending on which one you choose. Do your homework with a spreadsheet showing advantages, cost, and how many prospects you can add to your list—very important!

Landing Page/Squeeze Page Creator—You are probably wondering what is this. Well, it's fairly simple. It is a way for you to design a "wrapper" for your campaigns that will get people's attention! A lot of marketers don't use this tool, but if you want to be successful, this is a must! Remember this phrase: "Marketing is a contest for people's attention." This tool will give you the ability to do this correctly. Again, you can Google *squeeze page creator* and look at the various ones you may like. Word of caution: the "free" ones usually don't have the advantages you will need in setting up your campaigns.

Later in the book, I will discuss more on this tool and even have a great idea for you to review. But for now, this tool is a must for creating your great-looking campaigns that get people's attention to want to see more! You will also learn how to connect the L/P creator with your autoresponder, so building your list just got easier! Again, most all the squeeze page companies have pretty good video training explaining how everything works, so don't get confused with these terms and tools. They are fun to use to create your campaigns.

Tracking—Your results is very critical for your business because you need to see what landing pages are converting and what "percent" closing ratio you are getting from your campaign. To find a tracking service, once again, Google tracking/measurement devices and see if one fits your business needs. I have used two different companies, and both are very good, but there is a cost for both companies: Click Meter and Quality Click Control.

For most of my tracking, I am using Quality Click Control, mainly because I get excellent support on my campaigns and can talk to them at any time. Remember this: Unless you know your results, you have no way of knowing which squeeze page or landing page is giving you the best results, and it is impossible to set up effective campaigns for the future!

Traffic—This is the last tool you will need to start your campaign, but it is one of the most important ones. Without "eyeballs" on your offer or website, you have no sales! To start with traffic, sign up for all the social media programs: Facebook, Twitter, YouTube, LinkedIn, and Pinterest.

These social media programs are free and have a lot exposure if you market them correctly. I would also add *referral key* to your list of "free" media programs. These are a great place to start (we call them low-hanging fruit) because marketers usually get results right away without spending any money! Next, you need to think about *e-mail marketing*. This is what buys leads for a cost and sends your offer to the leads through a landing page/squeeze page.

You do this with what I call a simple script that you write in text form, always keeping your main theme of your squeeze page highlighted in your e-mail marketing campaign, saying something like this: "Tap Into the World's Largest Media Buyer List." This would be your header in your e-mail if it . . . Connects to your landing page. By using a headline similar to this, you will hold the prospect's attention.

Remember this phrase: "Marketing is a contest for people's attention." Always do your campaigns and text *totally different* from other affiliates, if you are in an affiliate program. You want to always "stand out." If not, you are invisible to your prospects!

There are many other areas of advertising you can use like OPL (other people's list), Google Ad Words (advertising on Google), CPC (cost per click) like used in solo ads; but for now, I suggest you stay with what we just covered before you venture into these advertising programs because if you don't understand them, you could spend a lot of money and don't know it! With any advertising campaign, always start small and then scale up after you see some results and have more experience.

Right about now, you are probably wondering, *Can I do this?* Let me assure you, yes, you can do this type of home business, and believe me, it's fun, really exciting, and has a lot of rewards, especially when you get your first sale! So my advice is don't get overwhelmed because I have seen newbies do online marketing and generate from $5,000 to, in many cases, $20,000 per month in sales in the first sixty to ninety days. I can't make you this claim that you will do this kind of sales, but if you are dedicated, follow the system and always look to further your education. With online marketing, your success will be amazing!

I want to give you a flow chart of what a typical marketer's campaign looks like and what yours needs to look like to crush your competition.

Typical Campaign

Landing Page/Squeeze Page → Sales Page

Using this kind of approach gives very little value to your prospect. It's like a take-it-or-leave-it approach. Now let's look at what I am recommending you do differently.

Advanced Campaign

Landing Page → Thank-You Page → Lead Magnet → Sales page

You may say, what's the difference? It is summarized here: The *landing page* gets the prospect's attention. The *thank-you page* thanks your prospect for looking, and you put even more support about your L/P. At the same time, it asks your prospect for their e-mail address. You are doing this to build your list through your autoresponder and saying something like this(Get Access Now) for more Valuable Marketing Secrets (Lead Magnet Page) then send them to your Sales Page . . . with a button that says (Click Here To Get Access) to world's largest

Media platform or something like this. Doing this provides value to your prospect.

Now don't let the information on page confuse you. It is only a way for you to see how to structure your offer, to "stand heads and shoulders" above your competition.

If you want your sales conversions the highest, then set up your campaigns like the prior page under advanced! Remember, you can also give away "free" stuff in the second example to give more value to your prospect, like free e-books or free lead sources. All you have to do is put them in your text in your lead magnet that would direct your prospect to your offer (sales page).

More about setting up your campaigns will be discussed later on in the book, so I suggest you read this material a couple of times so you will have an idea of how your campaign will convey your offer to your prospect!

Chapter 3

How to Choose a Product or Service to Promote as Your Offer

Choosing a program or service to promote is not hard as marketers would like you to believe. To me, it's "fun" because this is where you start your *real marketing*. Let's take a look at the types of offers you could promote:

Affiliate Program—this where you choose an offer from the hundreds of e-mail proposals you could receive every day. You also may know somebody who is in an affiliate program and they may suggest you try it. If this is the program you want to start, there are some critical points you need to answer for this type of programs:

1. Company—Has it been in business for over two years?
2. Compensation plan—Do you get 100 percent commissions? (Recommend this.)
3. Products—Are the products remarkable, and would people want them?
4. Marketing system—Is it defined, and can you "model" it?
5. Support/Training—Does it exist, and how often do you get trained?
6. Timing—Can the program go globally, and what is the vision of the company?

Really do your homework here, so you don't get any surprises. There are a lot of recycled programs that marketers are getting people into and wind up closing with the people losing all there investment!

Here is another thing to stay away from: programs where you have to build a large team (usually matrix commissions programs). It is way too difficult to build a team of dedicated marketers because you have to use selling techniques, and people just don't like "salesmen" or being sold. They would like to make up their own minds based upon the merits of the offer and whether it solves their problems.

Another point to watch is the "flashy hype" programs, in which they wear you down with hype—fancy cars, fancy houses, and you will be a millionaire overnight. They just don't work! Watch the earning hype programs, in which they keep showing you bank receipts. They are all staged!

Your Own Product Here—this is another way to set up a successful campaign with your own product. Some people buy items from Amazon and market them on the Internet. However, the commission or return of investment is smaller since you can't mark them up to make a real nice profit. There is another way of getting your own product to promote. Google, for example, top 20 trends of what people are looking for on the Web. See if any of these trends catch your eye and you would like to promote the issue. Let's take a look!

I am recommending you do this to find a product you want to promote. Go to Google, type in top 25 trends people are looking for, and see what you come up with. I will give you some examples. These are not in any order:

1. Marriage issues
2. Divorce
3. Facebook
4. Bankruptcy
5. Legal issues
6. Twitter
7. Adult content (don't use this)
8. Current events
9. How to make money online
10. YouTube

For example, if you want to promote any of these items, you would have to be very familiar with the subject matter, and research your idea so you can fill the need of people visiting Google for information on your product. I have known people who became experts on what type of dog they recommend and why and have made a good living online. Just remember to research your idea for your offer from A to Z so when you set up your marketing campaign, all the bases are covered.

Very successful marketers online are promoting their own products they have developed over the years, so if I were you, I would look at this very carefully. Remember, one idea can literally make you a millionaire overnight!

There is another way you can find products to promote, and it is by using ClickBank. This vendor house has thousands of products you can choose from and promote. Even though your commissions may not be as much, you can find products for anything you may look for. It's all here, and all you have to do is set up a free account and watch their video training programs to learn how to promote and market your offer. If you decide to do this idea, make sure you design your own wrappers and materials like we talked about in chapter 2 because thousands of marketers will be promoting the same offer as you, normally using the marketing promotions given to you by the seller. Therefore, you will all look the same unless you follow chapter 2 guidelines for setting up a campaign. Remember, when choosing a product, always choose the product that will appeal to people (prospects), like lose twenty pounds in three weeks!

Just a couple more comments on product selection, *stay away from low-cost products*. The commissions are too low, and you need thousands of sales to make some money. *Don't get swayed by the "hype" programs. Don't get into matrix-building programs.* The only people who make money here is the company.

Later in the book, I will be touching again on product selection and other important criteria on setting up a campaign, so watch for it later on!

Chapter 4

Picking a Domain and Hosting Account

With your business, you need to have a domain that you can use with your website and with your marketing campaigns. I use GoDaddy. First, set up an account with GoDaddy, and then write down about twelve to fifteen domain names you would like to use. The reason for twelve names is there is a good chance many of your choices are taken. All you have to do is search to see if your domain is taken.

Here are some examples of a domain:

1. financialfuture.com
2. makemoneyathome.com
3. weightloss.com

Try and use a name that connects with your product or campaign you plan on running. This way, there is a connection for marketing. I have a domain: TDE.rocks (total domination engineering) is one of my campaigns. Don't get frustrated if you can't use your first five choices. That's why I said write down twelve names or more. There are marketers who buy up domains and sell them back as a way to make a profit, especially if the domain is one that a lot of businesses want.

Before I go into *hosting*, you can expect to pay around $12–$18 per year for a domain, fairly cheap. Like I said before, I like GoDaddy because they have really good support, and you can even get them on the phone—amazing in today's business world! Remember, you can also use extensions other than *.com*, which is the most recognizable, like *.org*, and many more will be offered when you can't get your domain with *.com*. I use *.com* and *.org* with my campaigns.

Hosting—Once you have a domain, and it takes about twenty-four to forty-eight hours to register, you will need a hosting account, and I suggest you use GoDaddy for that as well. This way, you get amazing support and training! The purpose of hosting is to host your domain for your website or for your marketing campaigns. Not much cost here too, especially if you use the same supplier for both domains and hosting. GoDaddy has some great video training on hosting your domain, so you can't go wrong using them for both functions.

Chapter 5

Why You Need an Autoresponder

In this chapter, I will be discussing one of the most critical tools (a must-have) for your home-based business. Of all the tools, this one may be the most important.

Reasons you need an "autoresponder:

If you are going to build a list, ever heard of the term "money is in the list"? Follow up e-mails sent to your list at a scheduled time. You can even use it for newsletters sent to your list. Also, it is very good at retargeting offers to your list.

Back in chapter 2, I showed you a flow chart on how I recommend you set up your campaigns. It is designed for maximum results from your offer. There are many autoresponders on the Web that you could choose from. However, with experience, I have narrowed your search down to two companies similar in their design but different in applications. The two companies are AWeber and GetResponse. I use GetResponse because I have found them to be a little more responsive with support, a little cheaper, and you don't have to worry about losing your data (list) like AWeber had done in the past.

GetResponse also has a free trial period to see if you like their package. You will need to set up an account, regardless of which company you go with. After, go to their video training sequences for training. I would start with their package of about 2,500 prospects per month. This is plenty to start your list-building efforts with. Make sure you review their "spam" section. It will help you with your text content with e-mails, newsletters, blogs, and follow-up sequences for retargeting.

There are a couple of things I need to make you aware of when using your autoresponder. Always *connect* your campaign offers to your A/R, short for autoresponder, so you could build your list. Support will help you with setting up your connection correctly.

Remember to mention in your campaigns that prospects' e-mail addresses will not ever be given out to an outside service of any kind and will only be used by you to give prospects "free" value and notices of upcoming events.

Your autoresponder is so valuable you can even "schedule" mailings to your list for a particular day and time of day. Speaking of this, I always send out e-mails to my list on Wednesdays through Fridays, on a weekly basis. This is based upon surveyed opt-in stats. So remember this point in your follow-up efforts.

Another thing I want to point out is never bombard your list with e-mails. Always be creative and have a catchy headline to get your prospects' attention. I only send e-mails once every nine days and newsletters only once per week. They have no offers but valuable marketing information your list could model and use. Always remember this: Would you like to receive e-mails from various sources every day? Think about your prospect list the same way. They will respond better to your messages!

Chapter 6

Starting a Campaign

This a good place to talk about something that most marketers never mention or discuss, but I believe if you do this particular function and review your "why" every day, your focus will be so much better on your marketing, your advertising, and your campaigns based upon this known little secret.

This known little secret is "why." You're probably wondering what I am talking about. "Why" is very simple but very powerful: Why do you want to do this business in the first place? You see, "why" is broken down into two different categories:

1. Personal Why—Why are you doing this business—for more money, for more time with your family? Do you want better vacations, travel? Your personal why should never be about earning money. It goes deeper than that. For example, I have written down my personal why, and here it is:

ONE VISION

ONE MISSION

ONE GOAL

To be debt free in three years, have more time for my wife, have a new house in four years, help other people achieve their lifelong dreams.

I have my "why" on a card and look at it every day before I start work so I am focused on the task for today. Yes, a lot of people may say that's silly, but motivational speakers like Tony Robbins and Bob Proctor will tell you it works! You have to understand in your mind "why" you are doing this business, and if this keeps you focused, that's even better!

2. Business Why—Is it to reach your goals, be debt free, help people reach their dreams/goals? You can use money as a motivator in this why. As you will notice, I combined both whys into one so I don't have to carry two cards and can always refer to why I am doing this business!

This little secret will help you with the ups and downs you will experience in doing your business. Don't take this lightly. I know a lot of great entrepreneurs who use it every day!

Chapter 7

Your Why Is a Very Important Part of Your Goals

We just covered a mind-focused exercise called know your "why." Now we need to change our focus to measuring results from your campaigns. You can only have successful campaigns if you know all the results. Let's take a look at what you need to track:

1. You need to know how many clicks or opt-ins are you getting for a particular campaign. What I mean is the number of clicks or opt-ins or the number of visitors who looked at your landing page/squeeze page, whichever you use to call it. Now divide the cost of the campaign into the number of clicks you got. This gives you the cost per click. For example, you buy one hundred clicks for $60, and you get seventy-five visitors look at your offer. That is equal to $0.80 per click or opt/in. Did you get my example?
2. You need to track the number of conversions you got for the same campaign. You do this by taking the number of conversions (sales) you got. Let's say you got five sales. Divide that by your campaign cost, $60. That comes up to $12 cost per sale. Now let's say your offer sold for $45 apiece. This means you got $225 in total sales. Divide it by $60 in cost means you received $3.75 per dollar you spent. I would take that ratio in every campaign!

3. You need to measure or track the cost of building your list. Let's say you are just adding prospects to your list to increase your list size, keeping in mind the money is in the list. You spend $100 and you get two hundred opt-ins added to your list. Your cost per opt-in would be $0.50, not too bad, but the lower cost of adding people to your list is in your favor and if they are legitimate prospects with good e-mail addresses!

Let's look at some costs you could expect to pay today for different campaigns:

Solo Ads—The cost per click using this media runs anywhere from $0.30 per click up to $0.75 or higher. To make sure you are getting a good value for your investment using solo ads, always ask your seller if he thinks your offer (script) is what solo ad vendors use and whether it is a good fit for his list. Also, ask how many other offers like yours has he run through his list. If he says five or more, then his list is being bombarded by the same offer—no good. Find another supplier!

E-mail Marketing—This is very popular, and there are many publishers and sellers offering their services to anyone. The cost per lead will range from $0.05 to $ 1.00. Because there are many sellers offering this type of service, you have to be watchful that the sellers aren't using old recycled lists that are worthless. Always ask for people who use their service (leads). E-mail them for a referral on the seller. Because there is a high demand for "traffic," many marketers are taking advantage of this demand using old lists and making good money doing it. Later on in the book, I will address traffic again.

Google—This is, without any doubt, the most reputable media source on the Web, but people (marketers) are afraid to use their service, like Google AdWords, for fear of being banned in the middle of a campaign! Later in the book, I also have an idea for you to create campaigns with "no fear" of being banned by Google. It's priceless information and training!

Chapter 8

Tracking and Measurement—So Important

You have to have visitors to your website or landing page in order to make a sale! Buying traffic is tricky today because there are many more sellers making a living selling leads. Because traffic is so much in demand, many sellers are shady, selling old recycled lists from six years or older at your expense.

I am going to give you a few sources that I am familiar with for you to start with:

For solo ads:

Andrea Smith Fulton	adulton1977@gmail.com
Phil Springer	pstephenspringer@gmail.com
Randy Harris	solos@solosforsale.com
James Neal	realjamesneal@gmail.com
Jayson Benoit	http://jaysonbenoit.com/solo_ads

For traffic leads:

Jessie Sotomajor	http://www.1sttiertraffic.com

Social media—Facebook, Twitter, YouTube, Referral Key—This is where I recommend you start your advertising campaign once you have all the pieces in place. Not only is it "free" to set up an account, but you can also get some real good exposure for your offer. YouTube is basically for you to create a short video, say three minutes long, using your cell phone, being yourself, and explaining your product or service really works well. If you need more information on doing videos, you can always Google how to shoot videos for YouTube! Videos are well worth the effort because a lot of people like videos more than text. Just act like you are talking to a friend doing your video and have some bullet points in a place where you can see them but won't be in the video unless you are doing a white board.

I have listed just a few traffic sources for you to start with. However, you can also Google first-tier leads to investigate more sources. Whatever sources you start with, always start small. You can scale up your campaign later, but you are almost in a test phase. Remember, track your results. Later in the book will be more on starting up your campaign with different options.

Chapter 9

Traffic Sources—Main Stay of Any Campaign

I cannot stress enough how important it is for you to understand who your customer (prospect) is and what are his needs you need to solve. Ever heard of the term "who told you dreams come true"? This can only be true if you have the training and tools and support to implement successful campaigns. When you survey a number of marketers and ask them whether they make money online, the answer is "no" or very little money. It's true, only 97 percent of the people online make less than $100 per month! Why is that? It's because they don't have the *tools*, *training*, and *support* needed to be successful. If you follow this book and implement the ideas I have laid out, you will break that cycle and be successful like super affiliates are! Another reason marketers fail is they follow the herd marketing approach—doing everything just like what hundreds are doing. That too doesn't work. Again, the concepts outlined in this book will take you above the herd.

Only a handful of marketers really know what their customer wants. I want to come back to this in a few minutes, but for now, I want to give you some criteria used by successful entrepreneurs:

- Understand that people are ignorant
- Are you willing to sacrifice to get to your dreams?
- Are you prepared to fail before you succeed?
- Most successful marketers always start with something that is broke!

- If you don't have what you need, get it!
- The more you engage, the more you gain!
- If the ship sinks, build another one!
- Everything repeats itself in time!
- Do you realize that you are unique? No one else is like you!

Very interesting list. I got this from a very successful marketer who makes six figures annually and works twenty-one hours a week! He must know something that other marketers don't know. I suspect the answers are in this book. So don't be afraid to read it over many times!

Don't ever look at your business like a job but as a live entity!

Now let's take a closer look at what makes up your customer (prospect).

Customers all have the basic needs as pointed out by Maslow: air, food, water, shelter, warmth, sex, and sleep. But what are their needs as far as business goes? Or do they have pain you need to solve? It all goes back to what problems or pains they are having with a business or personally. This is your marketing assignment: Try to find out what is causing them concern in business or personally, and you come up with the "right" solution that solves their issues. There are many ways you can find out what concerns or problems they have. You can send a survey to your list, asking your people to list the three biggest problems they have. If you get the same answer over and over and over again, you will know that these problems probably exist in business or personally with a lot more people. Now you have a marketing idea for a product or service that solves the problems, and all you have to do is market it to your list and other traffic sources! Pretty cool stuff, or you can Google top 25 trends and see what you come up with.

Now we touched a little before on Google trends, but here are the top 8 trends:

1. Marriage
2. Bankruptcy
3. Love
4. Legal issues
5. Death issues
6. Family matters
7. Moving
8. Work-related issues

If you would like to use a marketing campaign to solve any of these trends people are looking for on Google, make sure you do your homework and know the topic from A to Z. Finding the right product or service to solve any of these issues will make you amazingly successful! You can also survey people on Facebook see what kind of problem issues they are having. Basically, you can survey on any media platform to get some ideas for a product or service you want to promote!

I can tell you right off that if you are looking for something in the business world to promote, then the top 3 problems that affect most all business are:

1. Need for more buyer traffic
2. Need for more sales conversions
3. Need for a better Marketing system

These are the issues for online marketers promoting some form of product or service. Now that you know the top 3 problem issues online businesses are struggling with, what do you do? First, find some effective lead suppliers and give the marketers one to two suppliers "free." You may have to ask them for their e-mail addresses if they are not in your list of prospects. All they have to do is give a correct e-mail address so you can send them the information. Giving them one to two always gives you the opportunity to come back with more free stuff or with an offer you are promoting for money.

When you do this free marketing of valuable stuff, you are branding yourself as a person of authority, which is what you want to be as a super affiliate marketer. Next thing you can try is giving away a free report, in which you give them a designed marketing plan that you copy from this book. You can also leave a couple of things out so you have more reasons to contact your list or network in social media with more value! I would give them the marketing plan of Landing Page—Thank-You Page—Sales Offer. Even though you have more ideas for marketing, start with this and fill in the blanks later on with more real value. Once people see that you are giving them value and are solving their problems, you got a customer for life! Are you starting to see how all this works? *Remember, the more you engage, the more you gain!*

Now before you start sending your campaigns with solo ads, e-mail advertising, or other advertising material, you need to do the following—very important:

- Have a defined purpose for your campaign (what are trying to accomplish).
- Set goals that are specific.
- Have a backup plan (like break glass here if campaign isn't working).
- Draw out your campaign in a step-by-step plan to accomplish your goals.
- Develop your marketing material and you are ready to start.

By doing these five things, it focuses you to review what you are trying to do with this campaign and to check your strategies and marketing material before you put your plan in action. By doing this, I sometimes find something I don't like and able to change it right away.

One other thing—*check your emotions at the front door*. Don't ever let your emotions run your business. Emotions change your "focus" on everything in your business!

Just a few more comments on this subject, marketers have a *fear of the unknown*. Instead of looking at this as a serious problem, think of your problem or issue as an opportunity to close the loop on your campaign. Close the loop just means you have looked at all the issues and checked your campaign marketing to see if it will do the job you set it up for. Never procrastinate with your business, and eliminate "two weeks" from your vocabulary, along with "can't do" and "can't do yet." Instead, replace them with a time table to accomplish your goals! You see, too many marketers and business people can't ever pull the trigger on their marketing campaign or sales campaign. They seem to be stuck with "I will have it going in two weeks!" This kind of thinking stems from "old habits" developed as they were growing up. Success will be failure if you can't act on your thought-out campaign. Always be positive, never negative. This will help you break some of these old habits.

Chapter 10

Know Your Customer

Before I give you a summary of starting your campaign, I want to talk about sales and marketing copy so you really have a thorough understanding of what your message needs to say with your wrapper landing page/squeeze page; so many marketers miss this critical point when they are trying to engage their prospect. If your wrapper (landing page) is focusing on solving a particular problem, then really point out "the pain" in your headline or subheadline. If you use the headline, then use the subheadline to amplify the problem. Then make sure you mention the solution to the problem, this could also be your offer, and finally, make the point. "Do you really want to continue what you are doing?" This may sound a little complicated, but it is not. Let me give you an example of what I mean (using weight loss as my offer). Headline: Are you suffering with weight gain? Subheadline: Has your weight gain prevented you from playing with your kids? Are you experiencing any back or knee problems because of your weight gain? Start losing weight today with this amazing new weight loss secret—three to five pounds per week possible, if you follow the plan! Do you want to continue as you are or change your life forever . . . now?

Do you see how I used the headline and subheadlines to my advantage, pointing out the pain the prospect is having and do they want I to continue or do they want to do something about it? You see this in every infomercial on TV. Just watch and see if you can pick up the points I outlined.

Now let's summarize your campaign. Let's call them campaign ingredients. First thing you need is a product you want to promote. I talked about it a lot. Next, you need a strategic funnel. This is your landing page, thank-you page, lead magnet (free offer), and your sales offer—product. Next, have your auto responder follow ups created and marked in the proper day for follow up. Next, have your strategic follow-ups in place with your autoresponder; we call this e-mail sequence. Now you have an idea of the tools (ingredients) that you need right now to start your campaign. You can always refer back to tools discussed in chapter 2 for more information. If you want to see a campaign in the shortest time, you need:

Product

Custom funnel

Autoresponder

These three things will get you started, but you will need more traffic for your offer, so refer back to chapter 9. Starting your campaign is the most exciting part because this is where you can watch and measure your results and be proud of your success! This is the where-rubber-meets-the-road metaphor!

I want to also make this point again: Never do marketing for the sake of making a "buck." Always have a purpose, a vision for your campaigns and how you are going to "help" people with their business or reach their dreams! This works hand in hand with knowing your customer, chapter 10.

Remember, if you find a solution for people's problems, or a least a segment of their pain or problem, it could be worth a "million" dollars to you! If that is not "exciting," I can't think of anything that even comes close! So let's get the marketing cap on and come up with the right product, the right message, the right wrapper and follow-up and have so great success!

Chapter 11

How to Set Up a Campaign

We have covered quite a lot of material in learning how to create a successful home-based business starting from scratch. Now let's create your campaign step by step! I am assuming that you have all your tools on board . . . So here we go!

Step 1—You should have gotten your domain and had it registered. Call GoDaddy to make sure your name servers are all pointed in the right direction for hosting your domain. This means you are ready. Good job!

Step2—Assuming you have picked a product or service or joined an affiliate program so you know what you are going to promote, design your landing page next. Key here is that your headline must really stand out, an attention-getter, same for your subheadline. Does the offer you are promoting solve the problem of your prospects? Refer to chapter 2 if you want to know more how your landing page should be designed. Remember, keep it short, simple, and to the point. Here is another example of a headline:

Make Money Online Fast!

Step-by-Step Training Free

Create $1,500 per month in 1 Week!

Click Here For Details.

Your thank you page can be created right on your auto responder. Go to the start-up page of your A/R. Go to top right-hand corner of the page. Click on your campaign's drop-down 'til you see "create a campaign." Type in your campaign name, hit "next," and follow the instructions. One more thing, go to your account settings, click on "permissions," uncheck all three boxes at the top of the page. This way, you will not be asking your prospect to a double opt-in. Next, go to the top of the page, click on "forms," create new. You will have two areas to select your forms/templates. Use the second. Any time you create a page of text with your auto responder always test to see if it opens by clicking on it. Be sure to test it to see if it opens. You can code this code with –(new) -you can copy this code for installation on your landing pages. Sounds complicated, but when you do it, you will see the connection between your landing and autoresponder. This is how they connect. Pretty cool!

Step 3—Now go to whoever you picked for your tracking/measurementcompany and go to the dashboard. Click on creating a new campaign. Follow the short instruction to get your tracking code. Make sure your campaign name is the same name you used with your auto responder. It will ask for a campaign name, same name you used with your autoresponder. It will then ask you for a campaign description. Use something like this: free traffic. Hit "submit" and it will take you to your summary page. Click on your campaign links and you will see the link that you should use with your landing page. When you set up your landing page, you will see an area called integrations. Click on this. It will ask for your autoresponder and tracking integrations. Just type them in or copy and paste. Remember, the tracking link you created is what you should use with your landing page. However, because it is somewhat long, when you are doing your landing page setup, use a button like this: **GET ACCESS NOW**. Highlight this phrase and go into your header information. Find a chain link. This is a hyperlink. Click on it. It will ask you for your link you want to promote. Click insert and your landing page now looks much better than the long code!

To make sure your tracking link works, test it by clicking on the "Get Access Now" button and see if it will open up to your offer. Your offer is the landing page you set up. If not, contact Click Meter or Quality Click Control and talk to support about the problem!

Step 4—Contact GetResponse or who you decide to go with for your autoresponder and check to see if your tracking link is also working with your A/R so you are building a list as prospects click on to your landing page. GetResponse is pretty good at helping find the problem, if one exists.

Step 5—Now that all your connections are up and running, it's time to get some "eyeballs" on your offer (landing page)! Let's start with Facebook. I assume you have created your account. Then go and post a catchy headline. For example, say something like this: "Create $1,000 per Month Using 3 Little Known Secrets." Learn how to do this in a step-by-step *free* training video! Link for access: https://tde42.com. (This is your link from tracking.)

After you have done that, do the same thing on Twitter, but make it shorter. You only have 140 characters to play with—short, simple, catchy! Then do the same for Referral Key. Wait for YouTube until you are comfortable doing a short three-minute video explaining your offer. Practice makes perfect in doing videos—practice but don't publish until you have the one you like!

With your social media, plan on creating a post daily this way you are branding yourself. By the way, do these every day—yes, every day—on social media. You are starting a personal branding of yourself and don't be afraid to change your wording every day.

Next, let's put together a solo ad. Go back to chapter 9 and pick a solo ad seller. Start with UDIMI.com and pick a seller you like and the cost you want to pay for one hundred clicks. Click on the seller and follow the instructions for one hundred clicks. It will ask you for a script. A script is no more than your offer. I would use either your headlines/subheadlines or some other catchy text about your offer. Don't forget to use your tracking link in your offer. If you can use a hyperlink, use it. It makes script look great.

Remember the points you need to ask the solo ad seller: Do you think my script fits your list? And how many offers like this have you run to your list in the last month? Just because you bought the solo ad doesn't mean you can't cancel it if you don't like what you hear from the seller! One final thought, go back to chapter 9 and see if you can afford any lead traffic. Even look at Leadmax.com if you can, and then look up some clicks (leads). Start small. Put together your short simple message, with bullet points to highlight the problem, and use a tracking link or hyperlink on the page. It will take your prospect to your landing page. Some marketers even insert some really neat pictures on this page for attention. If you want to go do this, go to these suppliers:

Can Stock Photo

Google free pictures

Shutterstock.com

Now check your results daily with your tracking provider. You're off and running toward success!

For reference, here is a flow chart for your campaign on how it should look when finished:

Traffic goes to your *landing page*. This directs them *your list*. The *thank-you page* directs to your offer. *Offer* directs to your follow-up e-mails, three in total.

Remember, your follow-up e-mails are designed to give the prospect more value about your offer, so really think this text through before you set it up in your autoresponder.

It looks simple, and it is if you have the necessary tools to get the job done correctly. Like I have said before, most marketers leave out some of these steps. This usually spells disaster for your campaign!

Chapter 12

Pitfalls *You Must Avoid*

If you hear marketers talking about why they are not making money online, it usually can be traced back to these points:

Hype programs—You see them every day. I usually get an e-mail box full of these every day, asking people to join their program using a lot of hype: fancy cars, fancy houses, fancy vacations done with hired actors. These programs never work because they are set up to where the company makes the money because it's too difficult for affiliates to duplicate or the commissions are so low you cannot be successful. *Don't get pulled into one of these!*

Remember the 80/20 rule. This means of the 80 percent of the people who get into a program only 20 percent will do the work. This is the same in any business, offline or online. Don't join a program in which all you have to do is recruit, recruit, recruit. Studies have shown people don't do well in this type of program. People are reminded that programs like this are focused on sales, and people don't like being sold or constantly asked to buy something!

Be aware of what I call the tire kickers. These are people who cannot pull the trigger no matter what. They have every excuse in the book for not joining or doing the work. It is always someone else's problem, never theirs! If you are building a team, don't put them on your team. They will spread negative thoughts throughout your team. Herd marketing—you have heard me mention this term in the book. A good number of marketers seem to follow the "herd" in their marketing efforts. Whatever other people are doing, they model. Nothing wrong with modeling a mentor or successful marketer, but I can tell you they didn't get success by doing what other people are doing. They did it by being different—standing out!

As you have probably noticed, nothing is "free" with online marketing. Just like in any business, nothing is free. However, you will be getting some programs asking you to join them for *free* and saying you will be rich in three to five months! Guess what, as soon as you join those programs, you will be asked to buy all kinds of stuff needed for your program to work. Don't fall for any of these sleight-of-hand offers. They don't work. People get frustrated, won't buy, lose their entry money, and the company wins! Online marketing is just like any business. You have to work it right, make the right decisions, have the right tools, and with dedicated effort, you will be successful!

Never forget that people are *people*, not numbers. They have dreams and goals just like you, so treat people with respect and value. Products come and go, but relationships last a lifetime! Remember, advertising is just a trait. Marketing is finding solutions to people's problems, relationship building, and storytelling!

I have been asked this question a lot over the years: How do I define "network marketing"? You will be amazed at my answer: recommending and promoting, along with building relationships. By the way, this is something you do every day of your life but probably don't know it. Let me explain. Do you ever tell your friends about a great restaurant you just visited—excellent food, amazing service? Do you think you are recommending? Same could be true for promoting a great movie or the best car you ever had. This is networking. Bet you never thought of it that way. So don't get confused or frustrated by the term or what people tell you how they see network marketing!

Another huge pitfall marketers fall into is their strategy is to "make a dollar no matter what it takes." Do you think they spend any time with building relationships? Do they try and solve people's problems and pain? No do-whatever-it-takes-to-make-a-buck! They will be out of business in three months getting into another program doing the same thing. Five years later, they are *broke*! Don't ever fall into that trap. Follow the strategies in this book and *success* is just around the corner!

Another big pitfall marketers do is not talking to their list. However, they will bombard their list with all kinds of offer daily. Just think about this: Would you, as a prospect, buy anything if you were e-mailed every day for some silly offer? It is better to send your list of prospects a newsletter or blog with value based material they can use in their business. You heard the phase, "Sow and you shall reap." Well, let me tell you, it works! Prospects would always like things of value than no-value offers!

I have said this before, the schedule I use for communicating to my list or prospects: blog, send once a week; newsletter, send once a week; new value offers, send once a week. If you have something with a time restraint, send it out accordingly. Always put yourself in your prospects' shoes when it comes to communication. They will like it and trust you more.

Don't you find it amusing that *competitors* are willing to share marketing stuff? I really find that amusing coming from the corporate business world, where everything secret was kept in a vault and only a couple of people had keys! Why do you think this happens in online marketing? Any idea? Well, it goes back to what I said previously, "you reap what you sow." This is only a pitfall when marketers are not giving "value" to their customer and prospect base. So always have this marketing concept in your campaigns!

The next pitfall I want to talk about is not having a "mentor." Almost 100 percent of successful people doing online marketing have or had some form of a mentor or a coach they could go to for answers and strategy when things are not going so well. Your learning curve with online marketing is like a Bell curve, so having a coach, who has done it successfully, is a must. Here is the big pitfall: The Web is crowded with all kinds of marketers claiming to be experts in online marketing, but remember, 97 percent of marketers make less than $100 per month online. *Do you want a coach like that?*

So the question is, where do you find a mentor? Well, if you are doing affiliate marketing, find the person or people who are doing the best in the company and start a relationship with them. Start by asking them marketing questions. They will feel important, and their ego will kick in, and you will have your mentor. Some programs will have marketing people built into their support system, but these are using high-cost programs. If you go to any annual gathering for your business, find out who the leaders are and establish a relationship with them. I know this sounds sort of silly, but I can tell you firsthand success comes from knowledge. What better place to get knowledge than from the leaders! Ever heard this phrase: Hang around with negative people and you will be a negative person? The same holds true for business. Hang around with the leaders, the ones who are making big dollars or commissions. Never hang around with the people who are failing! I am sure you wondering does this stuff really work. Just ask Tony Robbins or Bob Procter that question. The answer will be yes and yes!

As you become more experienced with your business, you will be getting e-mails daily from all kinds of marketers asking you to join their moneymaking offer and become rich overnight! I want you to remember this: There is no free ride to success. If you are in an affiliate program as a team member and you are looking for people to join your team, what is the first thing marketers do? They go and get their family members and friends to join the team! Now I don't want to sound negative, but this never works out. Your family and friends won't put the effort into growing the business, so forget this idea. If you need team members, handpick them after talking to them directly about your offer and your vision for the future. This way, you will get people like yourself dedicated to growing the business! Always stay away from the "slick sales" type of person. They are only interested in making a buck. Promoting your own product is where you want your business to go, now and in the future. That way, you are dependent on you for results. I hope this makes sense because you will also get more training in webinars put on by the company of the product or service you are promoting!

Chapter 13

Final Thoughts Before You Get Started

We have covered a lot of material in the book so far, but I don't want you to get the impression that this is a "hard business" to learn because it is not! The technical stuff in the book may seem difficult to understand, but once you get into it, it's not only fun but you will also want to do this business all hours of the night! Online marketing really gets into your blood, and you can't wait for the next day so you can design more campaigns, check your "stats," or look for more traffic sources.

Remember, online marketing is just like doing the things you are doing every day, talking to people, recommending stuff, giving your opinion on why this movie was the best, and it goes on and on. Focus on the four major ingredients we talked about:

Product

Funnel building (landing page)

Traffic

Follow Up

The rest of your learning curve can be picked up in webinars usually put on by the company you are promoting their offer or service. Always remember you can Google any subject at any time, even problems, and get ideas and comments, along with an explanation of your issue. Everything is at your fingertips!

I also get asked every week, it seems, whom do I recommend they go with to start a home-based business? I usually respond by mailing the person back and telling them to forget the product question. The better question is where can you get an educational platform to learn online marketing step by step!

You see, the product question is one you have to ponder on. Is it something that you feel comfortable with promoting and using yourself? You never promote an offer you don't use yourself! If you don't stand behind your offer 100 percent, this is a recipe for disaster! As far as whom do I recommend a newbie, and in many cases experienced marketers, use or go with, I can tell you from my experience there is only one company I would recommend; that company is HTA—High Traffic Academy.

If you are serious about making a home-based business into your primary business, then you need an educational platform where you can learn, experience, do campaigns just like the HTA affiliates do. The faculty leaders at HTA are truly amazing, and nowhere have I seen a more dedicated management team with a vision of changing online marketing better for people who want to start an online business! The expertise the faculty brings to their educational platform is the best. Nothing compares to what these people are doing and what their team of affiliates is doing. History looks like it will be made over and over by this team! Anyone interested in joining or looking at their platform, here are the links:

http://clikpms.com/75iwo14321k54pv (breakthrough engineering)

http://clpprms.com/rk5jpqfokokzehd

Link to join HTA:

http://clikpromise.com/5q4wfbllzt8p503

These links will give you a real good feel about what HTA has to offer and whether it will fill your educational needs. If you are wanting to start a unique business, I would have search long and hard for a better educational program on the Web!

This company is the only one that will give you a look behind the curtains at the most successful "Gurus". Where does their success come from? Can you model their success? The one thing that stands out for their faculty, they all have done the business at a high level and now want to share their successes with the team of affiliates—unheard of in any business! Remember to always treat your business like a live breathing thing, not merely a business. We touched on this before, having a positive state of mind will help you weather the ups and downs you will face with your business. If you are willing to do the tough things other marketers won't do, then success is just around the corner for you!

Never get off the course—always stay on the course you have designed for yourself in your campaigns. Don't ever let negativity in your business. This will spell failure!

You are embarking upon a new venture starting your own business, and I couldn't be more proud of you seeking another way of creating long-lasting wealth for your family and eventually your team. This will be the most exciting and rewarding time of your life!

GOOD MARKETING . . . GREAT SUCCESS. I hope we engage someday.

Sincerely,

Carl Kettenacker

BOOK SUMMARY

There are many books written on how to start an online business. However, none of them tell the real true story of what it takes to a "create" a new online business from zero to success like this book!

This book covers everything, from the "why" you need to start an online business to the tools needed for success and how you need to implement them, along with finding a product you want to promote and what you need to get started.

Topics like traffic sources, tracking and measurement, follow-up sequence are some of things you need to do to create you first campaign.

Every business has its up and downs, that is also covered in detail, and the most important aspects of starting your new business are discussed in detail. Knowing your customer, we had a great time discussing this very important part of any business, online or offline. We even went step by step on how to get started for maximum success.

www.ingramcontent.com/pod-product-compliance
Lightning Source LLC
Chambersburg PA
CBHW021048180526
45163CB00005B/2329